HOW TO PASS

STANDARD GRADE

DRAMA

David Roy

Hodder Gibson

A MEMBER OF THE HODDER HEADLINE GROUP

For Caroline

The Publishers would like to thank the following for permission to reproduce copyright material:

Photo credits

Page 19 (top) © Roger-Viollet/Topfoto, (bottom) © RIA Novosti/Topfoto; Page 20 (top) © Jorg Kolbe/dpa/Corbis, (middle) © Roger Viollet/Hulton Archive/Getty Images, (bottom) © Sucheta Das/AP Photo/PA Photos; page 21 © Richard Melloul/Sygma/Corbis; page 75 © Pir Foto/Phil Robinson/Alamy; page 87 © Owaki/Kulla/Corbis.

Acknowledgements

Extracts from Standard Grade Drama materials are reprinted by permission of the Scottish Qualifications Authority.

The writing of this book would not be possible without the assistance of the following people and organisations. To you all I give my thanks.

John Mitchell, Katherine Bennett and all at Hodder Gibson; Robert James; Newington College, Sydney; Gordon Jarvie of LTScotland, Brian Cooklin; the drama staff and pupils of Stonelaw High School, South Lanarkshire, SQA and my family Caroline and David.

Every effort has been made to trace all copyright holders, but if any have been inadvertently overlooked the Publishers will be pleased to make the necessary arrangements at the first opportunity.

Although every effort has been made to ensure that website addresses are correct at time of going to press, Hodder Gibson cannot be held responsible for the content of any website mentioned in this book. It is sometimes possible to find a relocated web page by typing in the address of the home page for a website in the URL window of your browser.

Hachette's policy is to use papers that are natural, renewable and recyclable products and made from wood grown in sustainable forests. The logging and manufacturing processes are expected to conform to the environmental regulations of the country of origin.

Orders: please contact Bookpoint Ltd, 130 Milton Park, Abingdon, Oxon OX14 4SB. Telephone: (44) 01235 827720. Fax: (44) 01235 400454. Lines are open 9.00 – 5.00, Monday to Saturday, with a 24-hour message answering service. Visit our website at www.hoddereducation.co.uk. Hodder Gibson can be contacted direct on: Tel: 0141 848 1609; Fax: 0141 889 6315; email: hoddergibson@hodder.co.uk

Impression number   5 4 3 2 1
Year   2012 2011 2010 2009 2008

Cover photo © Robbie Jack, stage lights © iStockPhoto.com/Joshua Blake
Illustrations by Richard Duszczak Cartoon Studio Limited and DC Graphic Design Limited
Typeset in Frutiger Light 10.5pt by DC Graphic Design Limited, Swanley Village, Kent
Printed and bound in Great Britain by Martins the Printers, Berwick-upon-Tweed

A catalogue record for this title is available from the British Library

ISBN-13: 978 0340 949 030

CONTENTS

Contents

CHAPTER 1

Introduction

INTRODUCTION

This book is designed for you to use on your own, without a teacher. It will help you to prepare for all the assessed parts of the Standard Grade Drama course.

This book is particularly suitable for you if you are aiming at Credit. You may already be earning Credit and wish to maintain and improve on the level of Credit you are achieving, aiming for an overall grade 1.

However, this book is also written to support students at General and Foundation levels who wish to raise their grades. If you apply the ideas here, and apply yourself in your work, you will succeed.

This book covers the three main assessed areas: Creating, Presenting, and Knowledge and Understanding. While these are assessed separately, to succeed at Credit you must try to apply all three together.

As well as learning how to succeed in the classroom, you will find advice to help you with folio assessment and the written examination.

There are examples, hints and advice throughout the book to help you.

Drama should be fun and stimulating to do. This book aims to encourage this and make it rewarding in an academic way. If you don't enjoy Drama that is the first clue that you are doing something wrong.

The Standard Grade Drama Course

What you will be assessed on

How is Standard Grade Drama assessed? There are three distinct areas for marking:

- Creating
- Presenting
- Knowledge and Understanding

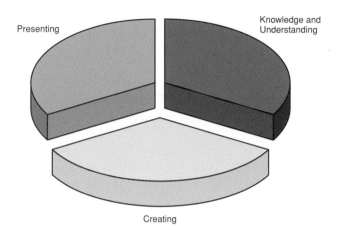

Just to complicate things, the folio will be made up of two essays that are only assessed in two of the three assessment areas.

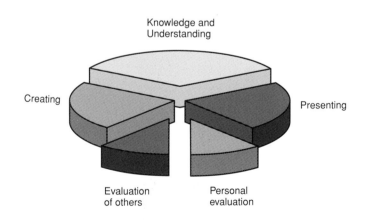

Creating and Presenting grades will be decided by your teacher about two or three months before your written examination which means that, by the time you sit your exam, two-thirds of your grade is already decided.

Finally, the exam that tests Knowledge and Understanding has three different papers: Credit, General and Foundation. You will be allowed to sit only two of the three papers.

If *you* are confused, imagine how your teacher feels!

Key Ideas

Before we start, there are two important ideas you must get your head around because they underpin the whole of this book: distinction and skills.

Distinction: There are three levels of grading at Standard Grade. These are Credit, General and Foundation. All pupils get to sit the General Level. You want to sit Credit, and this book aims to get you to sit that paper and pass. Passing is the difficult part. To gain a Credit pass, your work must stand out. It needs to show imagination and flair and be interesting to the examiners.

Just think about how much they will examine. You want them to sit up and take notice, and say 'That's different; that's great!'

Throughout this book there are examples and hints to help you avoid your work being boring and predictable and make your work distinctive.

Skills: There are few areas of Drama where there are set answers. Drama is rarely about learning facts; it's more how to apply what you know using your creativity and thought. You are being tested on your skills and knowledge, not facts. In this book there are plenty of techniques on offer to help you increase your skills.

Examining Drama

'How can I write about Drama?' you might ask. Drama is something done physically; it seems unfair to be examined in it. This is why there is continual assessment. Remember it was mentioned that two-thirds of your grade is already decided by your teacher? That is the continual assessment and it means if you don't work in class for two years you will not get a good grade.

Continual assessment

Your teacher is always watching you: how you work with others, develop ideas, rehearse, perform, assist others, and think about enhancing your performance . . . all of it. Teachers are often marking you even though you are unaware of it. These marks make up most of the Creating and Presenting grades in Drama. Your teacher has very clear instructions on how to mark you, called Grade Related Criteria (GRC). This means that students marked 500 miles away by another teacher will get marked in the same way as you do. Your teacher's marks will help decide if you sit the Credit and General examinations or the General and Foundation examinations. So you must start to work hard in S3 as well as S4. The information in this book aims to help you do well in class as well as in the final written examination.

The actual examination has two parts to each level. One part asks you to describe what you have been doing in class recently. The other part makes sure you have learned certain facts about Drama and you can use them on the spot, without preparation.

Remember there are no set answers in Drama. In fact, the end result of Drama may be important to an audience and make you feel good, but it is not the key part that decides your grades. The process you go through is just as important. Think about Maths – it is not only the answer that is wanted but the equations you used to get the answer. Drama is a bit like that.

All of this may seem very confusing so let's go back to the three areas: Creating, Presenting, and Knowledge and Understanding.

Creating is what you need to do first, and so that is what the next two chapters are about.

CHAPTER 2

Creating 1

CREATING 1

➡ Requirements

Creating involves the evolution of content and roles through practical investigation, experimentation and problem-solving. In this chapter and the next you will find information that helps you to do this.

What You Should Know ✔

What the exam board says about how to obtain a Credit in 'Creating'

The candidate can contribute a range of appropriate and occasionally demanding ideas; sustain fairly complex roles; and use space and other resources in new and inventive ways.

There are three areas:

Contribute ideas
in response to a stimulus, provide a range of appropriate and demanding ideas, most of which could be used in the creation and development of drama; in addition, expand upon and enhance the ideas of others by identifying the ways in which such ideas might further the drama being created.

Adopt roles
take on and sustain fairly complex roles, giving due consideration to aspects of role and relationship that have emerged; in addition, use language and movement at most times inventively and appropriately.

Use space and other resources
make appropriate and ready use of space and other drama resources, regularly identifying new and inventive ways of using both in the development of the drama.

There are three levels (Credit, General and Foundation) of Grade Related Criteria in each of the three areas but only the Credit definitions are given here.

What do the requirements outlined above actually mean you have to do?

Contribute ideas

This means you must work in a group and share ideas.

To achieve this you need to be able to:

◆ work with others and think

◆ listen to the ideas of others
    and offer ideas

◆ decide on what would be good to do and what would not

◆ note this down and remember the reasons for your decisions.

The great thing about all of this is that you are gaining skills that you can use in any job or area of life.

Having made decisions, you need to put these into practice.

Adopt roles

This means acting – becoming believable characters.

There is more on this later in the book, but a basic description is given here.

You have to pretend to be different from yourself by using:

Your body

Your voice

Your gestures

Your facial expressions

Use space and other resources

This means deciding on where to act and on ways to make it look better.

Here you need to think about the acting area, where the audience is and where the characters move on stage. This is different from adopting roles. In acting you decide on how a character acts. In using space and other resources, you decide on where a character acts. This can include setting in place and time, but also the reasons a character needs to be in a certain area.

Ask yourself why does your character sit on the chair, or move to the front. There must be a reason for this. This is using the space, often referred to as the 'blocking' of a scene.

You may also choose to use other resources such as lights, costume, set, etc. These are resources to help your performance work well. The more imagination you use, the better.

Stimulus

You were born with imagination. As a young child the simplest of things would let you 'play act' in another world. A box became a toy car, or a friend, or a wardrobe you hid in. As a child you had imagination. To be good at Drama you have to start being that child again and using stimulus to help you.

Every piece of Drama has to start somewhere. Stimulus is exactly what it states. It is something to stimulate your imagination, something that gives you a starting point that makes you think of lots of ideas. Sometimes it is a written script, and many plays you see at the theatre start this way. But it could be a photograph or a colour. Here is a list of the more common things that might be a stimulus for you.

- A script
- A photograph
- A picture
- An object
- A piece of clothing
- A phrase
- A sound
- A piece of music
- A poem
- A topic

In fact, anything that gets you thinking can be a piece of stimulus. You see, your imagination is important.

To help you start, trying the following.

Pick up an object in your house. Imagine how it could be used in an unusual way, e.g. a stick becomes a magic wand.

Now stop.

Why do you have the wand?

Where are you (use your imagination here)? Who are you?

When you start to do this you create stories and ideas, all started by a piece of wood. Try doing this activity with anything you find – create stories behind stories. That is stimulus and that is you on your way to being a successful Drama student.

Theories

How we turn basic ideas into a piece of Drama has had people arguing and experimenting for all time, but over the last hundred years some key practitioners (directors and performers) have written down their ideas or theories about this.

Names you might have heard of are Stanislavski, Meyerhold, Brecht, Boal, Copeau and Brook. Most of these people are now dead, and new directors and performers are offering more ideas.

However, the basic ideas of these six influential people are summarised here.

Stanislavski

Constantin Stanislavski (1863–1938)
developed a systematic approach to
training actors to work from the inside
outward. His 'System' focused on the
development of realistic characters and
stage worlds. Actors were instructed to use
their emotional memory in order to
naturally portray a character's emotions. To
do this, actors had to think of a moment in
their own lives when they had felt the
desired emotion and then replay the
emotion in role, in order to achieve a more
genuine performance. Stanislavski
proposed that actors study and experience
emotions and feelings and show them to
audiences by physical and vocals means,
also known as theatre language.

Meyerhold

A student of Stanislavski, Vsevolod
Meyerhold (1874–1940), put forward the
idea of physical style based on learning
gestures and movements as a way of
expressing outward emotion. He argued
that people feel physically before they feel
emotionally, so that, by practising and
assuming poses, gestures and movements,
appropriate emotions will automatically
occur. He developed a number of body
expressions, called bio-mechanics, that his
actors would use to portray specific
emotions and characters. He also linked
stage-set ideas to physical style and was
against trying to make physical style look
real.

Brecht

Bertolt Brecht (1898–1956) introduced the idea of epic theatre where, instead of the audience thinking about themselves being in the situation of the play, they were to have a view about the situation and question it and society; and then go out and change the world. To do this he reminded audiences that theatre was not real and that they were critical observers – he called this the alienation effect, *Verfremdungseffekt*. He used devices such as: actors talking straight to the audience; changing the text to third person or past tense; speaking the stage direction out loud; using exaggerated, unnatural stage lighting; using song; and using explanatory placards.

Boal

Augusto Boal (born 1931) wanted the poor to have a say in theatre and thought many plays helped promote the current governments. He created a political theatre and to do so he used many techniques that you also use in the classroom when Creating. Some of his techniques were: Forum Theatre, Invisible Theatre, Image Theatre, Newspaper Theatre, Legislative Theatre, Joker/Facilitator, Spect-actor.

Copeau

Jacques Copeau (1879–1949) was a French director who wanted theatre to become more symbolic and actors believable. He wrote a great deal about theatre and about training actors, believing in simplifying performances. His ideas have been highly influential.

Brook

Peter Brook (born 1925) is a current director who is internationally respected and has taken on board many of the theories of twentieth-century directors such as Meyerhold, Grotowski, Artaud, Copeau and Brecht. He believes in simplicity of theatre where the actor uses his body and the audience's thoughts to create imaginary and believable worlds that make the audience think.

These are very simple descriptions but you already do a lot of what these people suggest. You just need to remember why you do these things and you will pass Standard Grade Drama.

CHAPTER 3

Creating 2

CREATING 2

Themes and Plots

Anyone can create a simple story . . .

but there are two aspects to a story that make it interesting:

◆ what you say

◆ how you say it.

In Drama the 'what' is the message or idea or theme.

Stories should have a purpose – to entertain or inform, or both.

From the start you need to think about what you want say to your audience before you even develop a storyline. If you keep that always in your thoughts then your piece of Drama will be better and your grades will be higher. What is the theme?

To help you decide on your theme, consider:

◆ What do you want your audience to think about?

◆ It should link to your stimulus.

◆ It should be something you think is important.

Don't worry, though – just because your theme is serious, how you communicate it does not have to be serious as well!

Now that you have the 'what', it is time to think about the 'how'.

The 'how' has two parts: the story and the delivery.

Many performances (though not all) have a basic storyline. This is called the **narrative**. Again, keep it simple and believable: someone should be able to say

That could happen!

Key Points

Narratives can be broken into five key parts.

◆ **The Situation**. This introduces the setting, characters and what is happening. It is really important as it gets the audience interested in what is happening.

◆ **The Complication**. Here the audience discovers the key problem in the story and wants to find out what happens to the characters that they now care about.

◆ **The Development**. The complication and situation get explained further and the audience becomes even more involved.

Key Points continued ➤

Key Points *continued*

- **The Climax**. Everything comes to a head; the things that the audience knows about are revealed.

- **The Resolution**. Finally the audience finds out what happens to the characters and the audience feels the narrative has arrived at some sort of ending.

Most narratives have this structure – though they use different ways of telling it, in the **delivery**.

The delivery is the way you tell your story.

There are basically two things you can use to tell your plot and themes to an audience in a performance: theatre skills and theatre arts.

Theatre arts will be looked at in Chapter 4 on Presenting. In this chapter on Creating we focus on theatre skills, that is:

ACTING

Characters

To act, you must have someone or something to act – these are the characters or roles.

All characters must have some sort of name – even if the audience never find it out, the performer should know the name.

Indeed most actors create a **character card** for every role. They continually add to the character card throughout the Creating and Presenting process as they learn new things about their character during rehearsals.

Here is the basic minimum information you should include in a character card:

Name

Give a full name. Try to avoid joke names or famous names as these distract an audience from caring about the character.

Example

Name: Callum MacNeil (This name already tells us something about the character. It is a very Scottish name, actually a very common surname from the Island of Barra in the Outer Hebrides.)

Sex

This is important as some names can be chosen to fool an audience. Imagine that the audience hears about a character Jamie, and expects a male character. When we finally discover that Jamie is a female, it changes the story and can affect the theme.

Example

Name: Callum MacNeil

Sex: Male (This also potentially informs the actor of movements and mannerisms.)

Age

This will affect how your character does certain things and also their attitudes to certain things. The age should also be believable. It is unlikely that a character of 20 will be a Prime Minister, or that a 70 year old will be a computer game designer.

Example

Name: Callum MacNeil

Sex: Male

Age: 27 years old (This lets the actor start to decide about posture and movements.)

Marital status

'Marital status' is a strange phrase that means whether someone is married, divorced, separated, single, widower, etc. What has happened to a character in the past or indeed their current circumstances will affect how they behave.

Example

Name: Callum MacNeil

Sex: Male

Age: 27

Marital status: Single (This may now affect how he reacts to others.)

Job

Sometimes jobs are part of the story and sometimes they are not, but a character's job will change what happens to that character and how other characters treat them. Everyone does something. Even if they are not employed, they may be a student or a trainee. So, in this sense, jobs can include being a school pupil, being unemployed, or being a doctor, a teacher, etc.

Example

Name: Callum MacNeil

Sex: Male

Age: 27

Marital Status: Single

Job: Lawyer (This gives us certain expectations about the character and will affect how he reacts to others.)

Family

What family your character has can also affect them: for example, if you are a single child or the youngest child; if your parents are alive and/or together; if your family live near you or are far away; if you are a parent. All these things change the way you feel and how you react to others and events.

Example

Name: Callum MacNeil

Sex: Male

Age: 27

Marital status: Single

Job: Lawyer

Family: Mother and father, no brothers or sisters. No children of his own. (This character is on his own and has all the hopes and dreams of his parents to fulfil.)

Other information

You should also note down any other important events or things that the actor should know about the character that will make a difference to who you are portraying. Often a great deal of this information may be revealed during the performance, but sometimes it is useful just to invent these facts to make you believe in the character more, and get into the role.

Example

Name: Callum MacNeil

Sex: Male

Age: 27

Marital status: Single

Job: Lawyer

Family: Mother and father, no brothers or sisters. No children of his own.

Other information: Living in Glasgow, parents living on the Island of Barra. Working in a high-pressure law firm as a new graduate and wants to impress. Father dying. Callum brought up as religious, although he has rejected religion since childhood.

All this makes a believable character and informs you how to portray the character.

Reading the above example of a character, you might think that the theme explored in the play would be the conflict between family and work, because Callum will need to try to look after his family, who live far away, while making a good impression at the law firm. But this all depends on the setting of the play.

If your play was set 100 years ago, this changes things a great deal. Being a lawyer was seen as even more important then than it is now. Not practising a religion was very unusual and might be the theme of the play. Your play may also want to focus on a character moving from a small rural community to the urban city.

A character card is only part of a small piece in Creating a performance.

If you believe in the character, your audience will, and it will help you to pass Standard Grade Drama.

Body Language

Now that you have a character, how do you show or portray them?

There are basically two very different ways – through acting or through stylised movement. You can of course use a mix of these.

Let us focus on acting first.

Acting

A lot of people have thought about how acting should be done, and have had a great deal to say, as we mentioned earlier. One of the first to write ideas down about this was Stanislavski. He basically wanted actors to think like the characters and then reflect this in their movements. Others, like Meyerhold, suggested very different ways.

Here is just one simple way.

Start with your body.

Imagine you are your character and age.

◆ How do you sit?

◆ How do you stand?

◆ How do you walk?

Decide this and be believable and you will start to become the character. Copy people you know. Imitate them. Watch people in the street.

If you are playing a 30-year-old mother with two young children, watch different mothers with young children.

Ask yourself:

◆ What speed do they move?

◆ How do they open doors?

◆ How do they eat?

You will notice something important:

No mothers act the same way!

In fact no person acts exactly the same as another. If you think all police officers act the same way, or all truck drivers do, then you are thinking of a stereotype.

So whom should you copy?

Take all the pieces you have seen and learned and liked. Make choices. Consider which parts would suit your character.

Stylised movement

How do you think the character you are playing would move?

To help with this there is a movement breakdown called Laban (named after Rudolf Laban, 1879–1953, who was a theorist of dance and movement).

Is your character:

Open	or	Closed

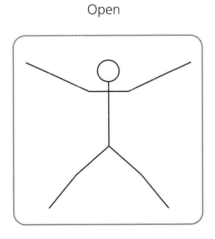

Angular   or   Curved

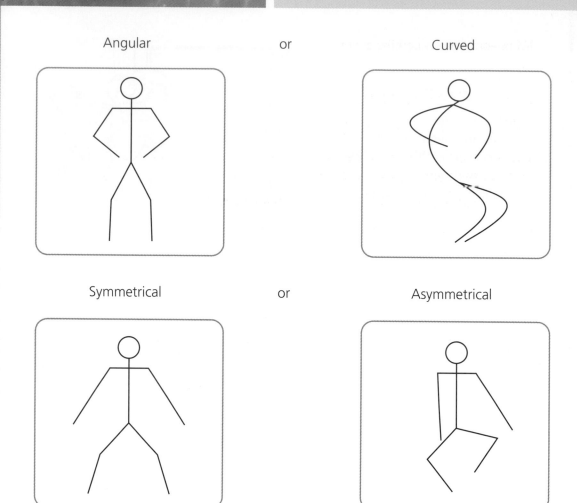

Symmetrical   or   Asymmetrical

These ideas will help you to become the character.

Now, in addition to movement, there is gesture.

How does your character use their hands or their feet?

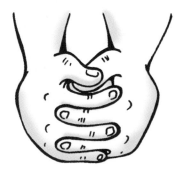

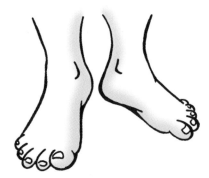

Think about the Laban list again.

Facial Expressions

Your face shows a lot of emotions and reactions.

A large amount of our brain's activity is focused on understanding other people's faces, so as an actor how you use your face is important.

Start to control the different parts of your face more:

- your eyes – open, closed, screwed up, etc.
- your eyebrows – amazed, frowning, etc.
- your mouth – wide, closed, tight, smiling, sad, etc.

As you can see, there is a lot to think about.

Mastering it will take time but remember: the more you practise and watch others, the better you will become.

Voice

You also need to start to think about your voice.

For the moment, forget about using accents; that can be practised later in your own time.

Your voice says a lot about how you are feeling. It can go louder or softer. In fact there are many things that can vary in the voice:

Key Words

ABC

★ Accent	Way of speaking used in a local area or country
★ Articulation	Clear pronunciation of words
★ Clarity	Clearness of the voice
★ Dialogue	A conversation between two or more characters
★ Emphasis	The stress on a word or phrase
★ Fluency	Natural, flowing speech
★ Intonation	Rising and falling of voice in speech
★ Pace	Speed of speech
★ Pause	A break in speaking; period of silence
★ Pitch	How high or low the voice is
★ Register	Appropriate speech for the person being spoken to, or for the situation
★ Stage whisper	A loud whisper intended to be heard by the audience
★ Timing	Speaking, moving or pausing at exactly the right moment
★ Tone	Changing of voice to express emotion
★ Volume	Loudness or quietness of the voice

On their own, each of these means very little, but when you create emotions and thoughts for a character that we can believe in, then you use some if not all of the above.

Think about how you speak in certain situations and emotions and then apply that to the character.

Example

Your character has rushed to see the king, to bring him bad news. His ruling has been broken and you were the sentry to discover it. You have done nothing wrong but are scared that the king will take his anger out on you.

You might use your voice in the following way.

◆ Your pace is fast because you are nervous.

◆ Your volume is louder than normal, but not too loud, as you are speaking to the king.

◆ Your register is polite and submissive.

◆ Your tone is worried and fearful.

◆ You intonation starts high on every sentence to show fear.

Mood and Atmosphere

Mood and atmosphere concern the feelings and emotions aroused in an audience by a drama. The key thing is how to do this through acting.

The first thing to be aware of is **tension**. Tension is the driving force of drama. It causes others to want to know what happens next, and it sustains interest and momentum. It prevents the drama from becoming boring.

Tension can be created through:

◆ Movement

◆ Voice

◆ Shock or surprise

◆ Silence

◆ Action

◆ Conflict and confrontation

◆ Mystery

◆ Relationship and status

◆ Threat or pressure

Theatre arts can also be used to heighten tension and create mood and atmosphere.

So let us look in more detail at some of these areas.

Relationships and Status

In every situation involving two or more characters, the characters are in a **relationship** of some sort.

For example:

◆ A waiter and a customer

◆ A husband and a wife

◆ A car driver and a police officer

◆ A car driver and a cyclist

Each relationship is different, and each 'role' in that relationship is different.

Again your character must think 'How do I feel about that character (even if they have very few thoughts about them)?'

A character may not have a strong relationship with a bus driver, but at least trusts the bus driver to have a driving licence. The knowledge of that relationship helps inform your character how to act and leads on to **status**.

Status is really important! It represents where, in order of power, your character is in any scene.

Imagine you are at school in a classroom and have done badly in a test. You have low status. This is because the teacher is in charge and you are not doing well.

However, you are also captain of the football team. The class think you are great because you scored the winning goal last week. You have a high status among the other members of the class.

Now you have broken your leg. You are in the hospital and people are gathered around you. However, it is your uncle, the doctors and nurses who decide what is happening to you. As you have no control over anything, your status is low.

Status can change in a scene, and different characters have different status in relation to each other in a scene.

Form, Structure and Conventions

So far, this book has been focused on acting. But acting is not the only way to develop a performance.

There are two key ways of describing a performance: form/structure and conventions. What are these?

Imagine a building. It has a shape – that is its overall **form** or **structure**.

The form of a drama is its overall style, for example:

◆ play, scripted or improvised

◆ comedy

◆ dance drama

◆ docu-drama

◆ forum theatre

◆ mime

◆ monologue

◆ movement

◆ musical

◆ pantomime

◆ tragedy.

The structure of a drama is the way in which time, place and action are sequenced. In a linear, or a chronological, structure the action unfolds from beginning to end. In a non-linear structure the action unfolds through shifts in time (flashback/flashforward) and/or place.

If the overall shape of a building is its form or structure, the pieces that make up the building are the **conventions**. When we look closely at a building, we can see that it is can be made of different bricks, wood, metal supports, plaster and lights: these are the conventions.

In drama, conventions are alternative ways of presenting part(s) of the drama, for example:

- aside
- flashback
- flashforward
- freeze frame
- frozen picture
- mime
- monologue
- movement
- narration
- slow motion
- soliloquy
- tableau (credit term for frozen picture)
- voice-over.

The different conventions are explained further in Chapter 5.

In drama a performance may have an overall form but can have lots of conventions to make it more interesting.

Blocking

Once you have decided how to use your body in acting, you need to decide where to move it around the performance area. This is called **blocking**.

You must decide *why* a character moves. There must be reasons or motivation for it.

- If I am hungry, I walk to the fridge.
- If I am tired, I sit down.
- If I am angry at someone, I might walk up to them, or away from them.

The actor will make decisions about where they go.

This is blocking a scene – deciding where and why a character moves around the stage.

You also need to think about *how* the character moves.

◆ If your character is angry, are all your muscles tense?

◆ Do you walk fast and determined, or slow and menacing, or in some other way?

You must decide this and know why!

Experimenting

All through the process described above, you should have been trying out ideas, some of which will work and some of which will not.

The key ideas you will need to consider when creating a role are summarised for you now.

Key Points

Creating a role

◆ What style of acting is suitable for this play, and why?

◆ What are the background, personality, attitude and interests of my chosen character?

◆ How is my character motivated?

◆ What is the role of my character in the play?

◆ What is my characters' relationship and feelings towards other specific characters in the play?

◆ How does my character progress and/or change throughout the play?

◆ How can I use my body language to portray this character?

◆ How can I use my voice to portray this character?

◆ How can I use gesture and expression to portray this character?

And as a director/writer of a scene, the key ideas to think about are:

Key Points

Directing/writing a scene

◆ What are the key themes and ideas of this play?

◆ Which themes and ideas do I wish to emphasise to the audience?

◆ Who is my target audience?

◆ How can I use actors to communicate my directorial concepts?

◆ How can I use the space to communicate my directorial concepts?

◆ What and how can I use other dramatic elements to communicate my directorial concepts?

◆ What difficulties does the text offer in communicating my directorial concepts?

Written Responses and Logbooks

Unfortunately, with all this practical work of Creating and experimenting, there is a downside. You have to write about what you have been doing.

There are two key areas of writing: the personal essay, in which you describe what you have done; and the first half of the written exam.

Both involve the same content; the difference with the exam is that it involves short answers to set questions, whereas the essay contains information in response to your own 'questions' (see the list below).

In Chapter 6 we will look at the examination in detail

The best way to prepare for the essay and the exam is to create a logbook and use it to record information. That way you have responses ready for the essay or the exam.

In your logbook for Creating put the following information:

◆ Your stimulus

◆ Personal initial ideas

◆ Ideas rejected and kept by the group, with reasons

◆ Basic themes and scenario/plot

◆ Target audience

◆ Characters in performance

◆ Personal character cards

◆ Rehearsal problems and solutions (try to keep about 10 of these)

Remember, this chapter has all been about how you create ideas. Once these ideas are formed, the next chapter deals with how to 'enhance' these ideas. This is called Presenting.

CHAPTER 4

Presenting

PRESENTING

Requirements

Presenting involves reviewing the results of the creating process, decision-making, rehearsal, presentation and evaluation. In this chapter you will find information that helps you to do this.

What You Should Know

What the exam board says about how to obtain a Credit in 'Presenting'

The candidate can regularly and extensively contribute to planning; can portray a wide range of characters of some complexity; can demonstrate considerable ability in theatre arts and technology; and can evaluate with some insight drama of self and others.

There are four areas:

Contribute to planning

contribute to the planning by regularly suggesting a wide range of possible ways of presenting the drama to an audience, taking into full consideration the constraints of space, casting, practical purpose and structure.

Portray characters

portray a wide range of characters, regularly and consistently demonstrating depth of character in accordance with planning and directing decisions already taken; in addition, show full awareness of audience needs by speaking appropriately, audibly and clearly, and by moving appropriately in the given space.

Demonstrate ability in theatre arts and technology

demonstrate considerable ability in theatre arts and technology in the use of materials and equipment for presentation.

What you should know continued ➤

What You Should Know *continued*

Evaluate drama
provide an extensive account of a drama presentation in which he/she was involved, judging with some insight the effectiveness of his/her contribution in the context of the group, and consistently justifying opinions and appraising quality; in addition, can provide a detailed account of drama he/she has seen presented by others, stating and fully justifying opinions on the effectiveness of the drama, with extensive reference to the performers and to the design aspects.

There are three levels (Credit, General and Foundation) of Grade Related Criteria in each of the four areas but only the Credit definitions are given here.

What do the requirements outlined above actually mean you have to do?

Planning

You must work in a group and share ideas. This is very similar to contributing ideas in Creating.

Now that your group has the basic ideas in place, you need to develop them through rehearsal and additional elements to improve your performance.

You have to work with others; sometimes you will not agree, but the skill of negotiating and arriving at a group decision is important.

If you are active in this process of negotiating you will gain high marks but if you sit back and just agree without any input then your marks will be lower.

Negotiating means you have to meet with and regularly discuss ideas with other members of the group.

Sometimes someone else can realise an improvement that you can not see. Any changes or developments should be discussed.

When there are disagreements, getting angry does not help.

You have to decide whether you want to do something because it is your idea or because it will improve the performance and therefore your mark.

Drama is not about showing off but about being the best you can be. Egos should be left at the door.

Portray Characters

You must perform believable characters that the audience accepts. Remember that an audience does not have to like a character for it to be one that works.

Having devised ideas for your performance, these make up the rough draft. Now you must develop your performance.

Firstly you must practise your ideas so that you stay in character. This is called **sustaining the role**.

To do this you must react and move and talk as the character all the time you are on stage. If you make a mistake, you must carry on and try not to be yourself on stage.

If you or someone else makes a mistake, try not to laugh as this is called **corpsing**. Basically, by doing so you 'kill' your character and become a corpse on stage.

The great thing about developing a character is that it is good fun to pretend to be someone else. You have to believe in your own character and in the characters of others. When you can do this the real fun begins.

Once you have established a character, and have made decisions about dialogue and blocking, you can experiment. In the early days of rehearsal you can try out various ways of doing things. Lots of ideas you try will not work; that is fine as long as you all decide what is best and works well. It may not always be the thing that is most fun but it should always be what makes the performance better.

Stages

You may have been rehearsing but you should also be thinking about the shape of stage you want to use.

Your teacher may tell you the type of stage he or she would like you to use. There are basically five styles: proscenium arch or end-on, thrust stage, extended stage, avenue theatre or theatre-in-the-round.

Proscenium arch or end-on

This is the most common stage shape used. It has an invisible wall between the actors and the audience. Stanislavski called this the fourth wall. It is a good stage as it allows the actors to have a simply placed audience, which means easier blocking. The audience is very separate from the actors. That said, this type of stage can keep an audience distant and can limit the performance as the audience is always fixed in one place.

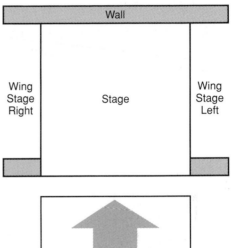

Thrust stage

Here the stage is built so that the actors push into the audience. It can make a more intimate performance and breaks down the barriers between actor and audience. Meyerhold liked this kind of stage. However, it can cause some viewing problems for audience members if the actors are not careful with blocking.

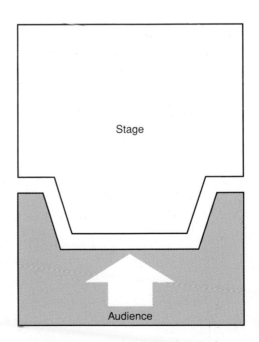

Extended stage

Here the stage extends at the sides so that the actors can almost surround the audience, and really break down the barriers between the audience and performers. The performers can almost intimidate the audience. However, some audience members will have difficulty viewing the performance unless they swing round in their seats.

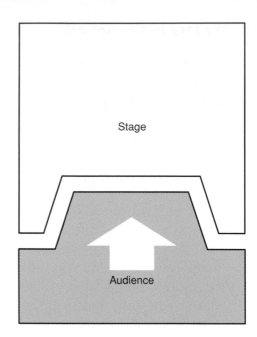

Avenue theatre

With audience on both sides of the stage, the performers are very close to the audience, and the audience are always reminded they are watching theatre. However, the audience will always have the back of an actor towards them and the set can be limited.

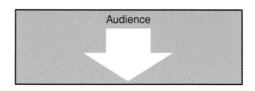

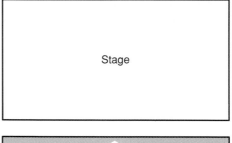

Theatre-in-the-Round

With the audience surrounding the performance, this is the most intimate of staging. It allows for audience/performer interaction. However, the performers have to work hard to allow the audience to have clear sight lines, and the set is very limited.

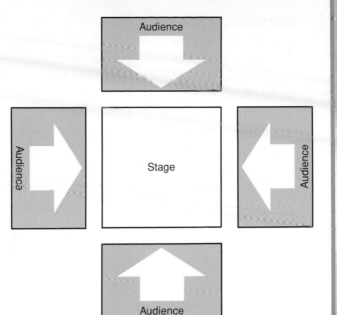

Theatre Arts

You have to show that you can use theatre arts and technology.

What are theatre arts? Theatre arts are often described as **production skills**.

These are the elements of Drama that are there to make an actor's performance look even better:

◆ Set design
◆ Lighting
◆ Sound
◆ Costume
◆ Make-up
◆ Props

What do the people applying these elements do? Below is a simple description of each of the production skills/theatre arts roles. How do you apply these to your performance? The resources and money available may be limited but there are some key questions you should ask yourself for each role, as indicated below.

Set designer and deviser

The set designer researches and plans, and often makes, the whole set (the area that the actors perform in). Set designers need to reflect the practical requirements of the play as specified by the script. They also need to reflect the ideas and themes of the play, as well as the style, period, setting and atmosphere. The set design should also be made in liaison with the director and should match his/her requirements. The set designer has to create the stage set, or source materials for it. This may include the making of a model as well as drawings and ground plans of the agreed set design. A key to the symbols used in drawing a ground plan can be found in the Appendix on pages 97-98.

Key Points

◆ What set requirements are in the script for style, period, atmosphere and setting?

◆ What limitations/requirements does my chosen performance area have?

◆ What additional requirements do other production team members have?

◆ What research do I need to do for the style, period, atmosphere and setting?

◆ What requirements does the structure of the play give?

◆ What materials will I need to create my design concepts?

Lighting designer and technician

The lighting designer chooses the types of lights, with effects and colours to reflect the time/place of action. Lighting designers also have to emphasise particular moments and areas, create mood and tension, and reflect the ideas and themes of the play. They should work in consultation with the director and stage designer. They need to list their tasks and the preparation necessary and have an accurate lighting plot.

Key Points

◆ What lighting requirements are in the script for content, style, period, atmosphere and setting?

◆ What limitations/requirements does my chosen performance area have?

◆ What additional requirements do other production team members have?

◆ What special effects are desired?

◆ What additional design style do I wish to apply to create particular periods, atmosphere, setting and mood?

Sound designer and technician

All sound effects and music are the sound designer's responsibility. Sound designers must look at the requirements of the play in terms of content, style, period, atmosphere and setting. They should work in consultation with the director. They should list their tasks and preparation for their role, and their responsibilities, and have an accurate sound plot, including music (pre-show and incidental if used), effects, and source, volume and duration of cues.

Key Points

- What sound requirements are in the script for content, style, period, atmosphere and setting?
- What limitations/requirements in equipment/materials does my chosen performance area have?
- What additional requirements do other production team members have?
- What special effects are desired?
- What additional effects do I wish to create in terms of particular periods, atmosphere, setting and mood?

Costume designer and wardrobe manager

All clothing worn on the stage must be chosen or designed specifically for the performance. It should reflect the style and period of the piece. It should also reflect the design concepts as already discussed in consultation with the director. Costume designers need to keep notes and/or drawings to interpret the script. They should list their tasks and preparation for their role and responsibilities, and produce final costume designs.

Key Points

- What costume requirements are in the script for characters, style, period and setting?
- What additional requirements do other production team members have?
- What research do I need to do for the characters, style, period and setting?
- What requirements does the structure of the play give?
- What materials will I need to create my design concepts?

Make-up designer and artist

The make-up artist designs suitable make-up and hairstyles for the actors, to reflect their character, status, background and themes of the play. Make-up artists may need to consult with the director and the costume designer. They should list their tasks and preparation for their role and responsibilities, and have final agreed designs/charts for all character make-ups.

Key Points

◆ What make-up requirements are in the script for characters?

◆ What additional requirements do other production team members have?

◆ What research do I need to do for the characters?

Props designer and manager

The person in charge of the properties (props) has to decide the requirements for the play. They have to decide which props are suitable and would enhance the production. They need to decide what style the props should have, in consultation with the designer and/or director and/or actors. They should list their tasks and preparation for their role and responsibilities, and they should have a master props list including all personal, set and costume props.

Key Points

◆ What props requirements are in the script for quantity, style, period and setting?

◆ What additional requirements do other production team members have?

◆ What research do I need to do for the style, period, size and setting?

◆ How would I best organise all personal, set and costume props?

Any or all of these roles can improve a performance. If possible, you should experience each of these during your course.

Evaluation

You need to comment on the performance and the process. As always you will be asked to reflect on what you have done.

In Creating you were asked to keep a logbook. The same applies here.

The Presenting element of the logbook should contain the following:

Key Points

- ◆ Diary entries – keep at least 10 for rehearsals. State the aim of each rehearsal, what was done, what difficulties arose, what solutions were found and what the aims for the next rehearsal were.

- ◆ Lighting ideas – write down either what lighting you are using for the performance or what lighting you would like to have.

- ◆ Sound – write down either what sound you are using for the performance or what sound you would like to have.

- ◆ Costume – write down either what costumes you are using for the performance or what costumes you would like to have.

- ◆ Make-up – write down either what make-up you are using for the performance or what make-up you would like to have.

Key Points continued ➤

> **Key Points** *continued*
>
> ◆ Props – write down either what props you are using for the performance or what props you would like to have.
>
> ◆ Technical rehearsal – Comment on how it went, what worked, what did not work and what changes you are making.
>
> ◆ Dress rehearsal – Comment on how it went. Be honest in your answer and try to give reasons.
>
> ◆ Performance – Try to comment on the positives and the areas you would now change. Often an audience can change completely how you think a scene might go. Comment on that, your own performance and the performance of others. Be fair but honest, and always try to justify what you think. Don't forget to include what audience members thought of the performance if you can.

Some of the props and costumes you might be able to organise by borrowing, some you might buy, some you might make, and finally there will be some things you can not obtain. Try to include that information in the logbook as well.

Assessment

You need to complete at least one essay, which is an evaluation of the performance of others.

The essay should show best evidence of your ability to give an account, to reflect, to appraise, to use relevant vocabulary and to justify the opinions given.

This essay is very similar to the essay for Creating.

Comment on the following:

◆ The plot/narrative and themes
◆ Casting
◆ Acting
◆ The set design
◆ Use of lighting
◆ Use of sound
◆ Costume
◆ Props
◆ Stage management
◆ Publicity and programme

Finally, give your own personal opinion on the performance.

Remember

Although you may not like something, you might still appreciate the talent and skills involved.

For example, I may not like a sport team who beats my favourite team, but I can still realise that they played better and showed more skill.

Be honest in your evaluation of another performance and try to justify your answers.

Example

A bad evaluation:

I liked the play. It was really well acted and the actors really suited their roles. The lighting was exciting and the costumes were really colourful.

The following is a very brief, good evaluation – yours would have to be much longer.

Example

The play really made me think about the issue of loneliness. It involved a child being evacuated from the city and having to cope with being away from her parents. Julie Smith was very believable as the 12-year-old girl, even although she was much older than this. She moved like a scared teenager, and her language made me believe that she was young and that she lived in 1941.

The set was simple, with two wooden crates, but the performers managed to make me believe these represented different areas just by how they used them and how they were placed on the stage.

Example continued ➤

Example *continued*

The sound effects really helped in this by creating areas that suddenly made me feel I was on a train or in an old shed. This made up for the fact that there were no lighting effects, as the performance was put on in the school gym.

The costumes were kept very simple with characters dressed in black and adding one piece of costume to become a character. One character had a jacket on to show they were an official, and then changed into a simple woollen jumper to become a farmer. I would have liked to see more detailed costumes from the period but the simple costumes meant there were quick scene changes.

I have never really been very interested in history. However, the play gave me a better understanding of how hard it must have been for young people during the Second World War. While the play was not my style, it was well acted and very clear in its message. This was shown by the full attention given by my whole year group as we watched it.

Presenting is also assessed through the second half of the written exam.

Once again the exam consists of short answers to questions, and the essay presents answers to your own 'questions'.

The best way to prepare for them is the logbook of your Presenting. That way you have responses ready for the essay or the exam.

In a later chapter we will look at the examination on its own.

CHAPTER 5

Knowledge and Understanding

Chapter 5

KNOWLEDGE AND UNDERSTANDING

Requirements

Knowledge and Understanding involves obtaining the information, experience and skills, through learning tasks in drama and theatre, and by the application of these to the practical situation.

In this chapter you will find information that helps you to do this.

What You Should Know

What the exam board says about how to obtain a Credit in 'Knowledge and Understanding'

The candidate can given a detailed and highly developed exposition of his/her ways and means of translating a stimulus into a presentation, with full justification for decisions taken.

There are three areas:

Respond to a stimulus
outline a situation of some complexity, originality and depth suitable in most or all respects for acting out, showing a developed awareness of drama form and structure.

Outline a character
provide extensive relevant information about a selected character with full awareness of the character's role and status in the drama.

Develop the drama for presentation
give in extended detail an account of his/her experience of drama, describing how the drama might be presented, with extensive reference to target audience, type of staging and technical aspects, and with full justification for decisions taken.

There are three levels (Credit, General and Foundation) of Grade Related Criteria in each of the three areas but only the Credit definitions are given here.

What do the requirements outlined above actually mean you have to do?

Respond to a stimulus

You can show that you have had ideas from the stimulus given for the exam. You have already shown this when developing ideas for Creating.

Remember the logbook mentioned earlier. This is where you will really use it. All your notes and ideas are in the logbook and you can use them for writing written responses, particularly for the exam.

How to answer the exam properly will be dealt with in the next chapter.

Outline a character

You must be able to offer detail on any characters you have created.

Remember that an audience does not have to like a character for it to be one that works.

If you have done the Creating process correctly, as outlined in Chapters 2 and 3, then you have already:

◆ considered and noted down the role and status of a character

◆ created a full and detailed character card.

You have therefore already produced all the detail you need for your characters.

Develop the drama for presentation

You must be able to explain clearly how you rehearsed a performance and applied theatre arts/presentation skills.

Again, if you applied knowledge and undertook the tasks in Chapter 4 on Presenting then your logbook for Presenting already has this information.

Form and Structures

As stated in Chapter 3, there are different forms and structures you can use. Here is a reminder of the different forms you can use, with some more detailed definitions.

Key Words

Drama forms

★ **Play, scripted or improvised – dialogue, with characters and a narrative**

★ **Comedy – a drama which is funny/comical**

★ **Dance drama – a drama presented through dance movements**

★ **Docu-drama – a documentary style of drama with reconstruction of events**

★ **Forum theatre – a play where the audience suggests changes to affect the outcomes**

★ **Mime – stylised movement which creates an illusion of reality**

★ **Monologue – a character speaks their thoughts aloud**

Key Words continued ➤

A B C

Key Words *continued*

* ★ **Movement** – use of the body as the sole means of communication

* ★ **Musical** – drama including song

* ★ **Pantomime** – Christmas theatrical entertainment usually based on a fairytale

* ★ **Tragedy** – a drama about unhappy events and with a sad ending

Structure is the way in which time, place and action are sequenced.

◆ In a linear, or chronological structure, the action unfolds from beginning to end.

◆ In a non-linear structure, the action unfolds through shifts in time and/or place.

Conventions are alternative ways of presenting part(s) of a drama. Again, here is a summary of different conventions mentioned earlier, with more detailed definitions.

A B C

Key Words

Drama conventions

* ★ **Aside** – a remark to the audience only

* ★ **Flashback** – acting out an event in the past

* ★ **Flashforward** – acting out a future or imagined event

* ★ **Freeze frame** – an action frozen in time

* ★ **Frozen picture** – an image, created on stage, held without movement

* ★ **Mime** – stylised movement which creates an illusion of reality

* ★ **Monologue** – when a character speaks their thoughts aloud

* ★ **Movement** – use of the body as the sole means of communication

* ★ **Narration** – when parts of the story are told as a story by a narrator

Key Words *continued* ➤

> **Key Words** *continued*
>
> ★ **Slow motion** – movement performed at a slowed-down speed
>
> ★ **Soliloquy** – a lengthy speech made when no other characters are on stage
>
> ★ **Tableau (Credit term for frozen picture)**
>
> ★ **Voice-over** – recorded speech played during a drama

If you have done the Creating and Presenting elements properly, then you have also done the Knowledge and Understanding element as well.

Theatre Arts Definitions

As explained in Chapter 4, theatre arts is the collective name for lighting, sound, costume, props, make-up and set. Here we summarise and explain the key words in each of the categories.

Stage management/general

★ **Apron** – a part of the stage projecting towards or into the auditorium

★ **Auditorium** – the part of the theatre designed to accommodate the audience

★ **Centre line** – an imaginary line running from the front to the back of the stage through the exact centre of the proscenium arch

★ **Centre stage** – the middle of the acting area

★ **Flat** – a flat piece of scenery lowered onto the stage

★ **Fly** – a large space above the stage from which the scenes are controlled

★ **House curtain** – the main front curtain in a proscenium theatre (see tabs)

★ **Marking** – marks indicating the position of scenery or props on the stage floor, usually with different coloured tapes to avoid confusion

* Offstage – backstage area outside the performance area

* Onstage – inside the acting area

* Opposite prompt (OP) – the right-hand side of the stage as viewed by the cast

* Orchestra pit – the sunken area in front of the stage where the orchestra plays during a performance

* Stage brace – portable support for flats

* Strike – clear the stage of scenery and other materials, or remove a specific article

* Tabs – a pair of curtains which overlap at centre, and together are the full width and height of the stage; front tabs are the house curtain

* Talkback – a system of two-way communications among the performance crew, each of whom wears a set of headphones with or without a boom microphone; also called cans

* Trap – a trap door opening into the area below stage, which can be used for special effects

* Wings – the sides of the stage concealed from the audiences' view

Set design

* Back cloth – cloth, usually painted, suspended from the flys at the rear of the stage

* Bar – horizontally flown rod (usually metal) from which scenery, lighting, and other equipment is suspended

* Cloth – area of scenic canvas hanging vertically

* Cyclorama – a plain screen with a uniform surface extending around and above the stage

* Downstage – the part of the stage closest to the audience

★ Entrance – a place on a set through which the actor may appear on the stage

★ Exit – a place on a set through which the actor may leave the stage

Lighting

★ Blackout – when the acting area is not lit

★ Slow fade – when the lighting is faded out slowly

★ Fast fade – when the lighting is faded out quickly

★ Snap – when blackout is achieved instantly

★ Crossfade – the change from one lighting state to another, with no blackout in between

★ Flood – a lantern giving a wide, unfocused spread of light

★ Focusing – positioning lanterns to create the desired effect onstage

★ Gel – film placed in front of a lantern to change the colour of the light beam

★ Follow spot – powerful spot used to follow actors around the stage

★ Fresnel spot – lantern giving a soft-edged beam of light with limited focus ability

★ LFX – the quick way to write 'lighting effects'

★ Lighting desk – control board for lighting

★ Profile spot – lantern giving a hard-edged beam of light

★ Wash – when the whole stage is evenly lit

★ Barndoors – adjustable metal flaps attached to the front of a lantern, to shape the beam of light

★ Safety chain – legally required wire chain that wraps between lanterns and bars as added safety

★ G-clamp – clamp used to secure a lantern to a lighting bar or stand

★ Gobo – thin metal plate cut out in a pattern and placed in a lantern to project a pattern or shape onto the stage

★ Special effects – used to create a mood or atmosphere onstage, such as a strobe light, mirror ball, smoke machine, stage fireworks

Sound

★ Cue – a signal for a sound effect to begin or end

★ Fade in – bring the volume up

★ Fade out – bring the volume down

★ Crossfade – change from one sound to another, with no silence in between

★ Live (SFX) – when an SFX is operated on cue during the performance

★ Pre-recorded (SFX) – when an SFX is recorded on tape (or equivilant) and played on cue during the performance

★ Music – an excellent way of adding to the emotion of a scene; can be live or pre-recorded or a mix of both

★ SFX – the quick way to write 'sound effects'

★ Mixing desk – control desk for sound

Costume

★ Costume – clothes worn by actors for their character

★ Hats – items worn on the head in keeping with the character being played

★ Jewellery – items worn on the ears, neck or wrists in keeping with the costume worn

★ Wigs – artificial hair in a variety of colours and styles

★ Costume list – a list of all costumes for each character in a drama

★ Period costume – costume which reflects clothing from a time in history

Props (Properties)

★ Props – (short for properties) items used or carried by an actor, or items on the set

★ Personal prop – an item carried or worn by an actor (e.g. glasses, wallet, mobile phone)

★ Set prop – an item placed on the set, usually part of it (e.g. lamp, clock, picture)

★ Props table – table offstage on which all props are placed for actors to collect as they enter and replace as they exit

Make-up

★ Fake blood – powder, liquid or capsules which create the effect of bleeding

★ Foundation – face make-up to create a basic skin colour

★ Liners – sticks of make-up in different colours used to create lines, bruises, shading

★ Scarring – scars created with make-up, putty or scarring material

★ Stipple sponge – sponge used to create an unshaven look or the appearance of cracked veins

★ Tooth varnish – varnish used to create the look of a missing tooth by blacking out an existing one

★ Crepe hair – plaits of artificial hair which can be cut and trimmed to form eyebrows, moustaches and beards

★ Nose putty – type of clay used for altering the shape of the nose or chin and/or making warts and wounds

★ Skull cap – plastic head-shaped covering to give appearance of baldness

As part of theatre arts, there are some additional topics that you may benefit from studying in more detail: masks and melodrama.

Both these involve acting techniques and so could be applied in Creating or Presenting. There are also many other acting styles which can be used. Indeed we have already touched on some of these in the section on body language.

Masks

The earliest indications of the use of masks in performance come from cave paintings in Africa, where a mask was used to disguise the hunter.

In Ancient Greek religious festivals, masks were used to exaggerate and accentuate the characters' features as well as to make the actors more visible to the audience.

Masks are extensively used in Asia, India and Africa in relation to dance, and also in carnivals and parties. Here the mask's interest is not so much to do with the character as with the idea of mystery, intrigue and disguise.

Neutral masks are masks that are plain in colour and do not show a particular or distinctive personality. They are excellent to use when experimenting, as their neutral quality allows the actor to explore a character. The neutral mask encourages the performer to be more expressive with their body language, as facial expression can not be used and voice expression can sometimes be limited.

It is often useful to practise with a mask by using a mirror so that you can view your ideas. This helps to make you keep the mask face towards one direction (such as the audience). You will discover what movement and gesture give a mask strength and what weakens the power of the mask. On key thing is to try not to touch the mask.

Greek theatre used full-face masks, but they were not neutral. They had fixed, exaggerated expressions, and the actors (who included a chorus) used very clear and precise movements. The chorus moved and spoke in unison and so created a very large visual style that could be compared to dance.

Commedia dell'arte

Half-masks became popular as they allowed for very clear voice as well as the extreme movements that mask work encourages. *Commedia dell'arte*, meaning the comedy of art, is the best known type of theatre that uses half-masks. It was most popular in Italy in the sixteenth and seventeenth centuries, The actors used half-masks to portray stock characters, characters that everyone in the audience was familiar with.

Each mask had a personality type, and the features of the mask highlighted the comic aspects of the characters. The actors and audience knew the different characters, which were always the same, even in different stories. (This is similar to some television 'soap operas' that you may watch.) The stories often made fun of local personalities and had some rude humour to them. Today we watch pantomimes, which originate from *commedia dell'arte*.

An important part of every play, given always to the most expert and popular actors, were the humorous interruptions, called Lazzi, which often had nothing to do with the play itself. They might involve clever pantomimic acting, acrobatic feats, juggling or wrestling, performed by a host of comic characters, often collectively called Zanni.

The characters

Arlecchino is the head Zanni but is still only a servant. Much of the humour comes from his plans and schemes. The character is a lot like a cat, and this is portrayed through his mask. The features of the mask show cat-like qualities, as do the actions of the character. Arlecchino is also led by his nose, meaning that his head turns first and then the rest of the body follows after.

Pantalone is the old man, who hoards all of his money. Being one of the masters, he is able to control the Zanni with the promise of money, even though he very rarely pays them. Pantalone is portrayed as a turkey or some similar bird – because of the way he walks, bent over and neck sticking out like a turkey. This was often played up as it allowed for lots of jokes and tricks to be played on him. His mask had a big nose that looked like a beak and long bushy eyebrows to give the character the illusion of age.

El Capitano, the mighty Captain, is the greatest warrior in the known world and also the greatest womaniser ever known, or so he says. This character is like a peacock, strutting around and talking about his achievements but, if anything happens, he will be the first to flee. His mask often had a long nose to make him seem manlier. He was often seen in profile with a pelvic thrust forward and nose pointing into the air at 45 degrees, while also pointing in the same direction with his sword or slapstick. This poise was generally used when explaining what his achievements were and what he would do.

The lovers are the only characters that are not masked, as their beauty is natural, applied only with make-up. They are often the centre of the other characters' interests as they are easily manipulated, being only concerned with their love for each other and not caring about anything else. One interesting feature about the lovers is that they never touch, even in the most passionate moment. They would come very close to each other, in dramatic poses, but wouldn't touch, as though if they did it would destroy anything that had happened.

Melodrama

Melodrama was once the most popular form of theatrical entertainment. It reached the peak of its popularity in the mid to late nineteenth century.

Melodrama helps us to understand the influences of melodramatic plots on films and television today.

Melodrama was emotional theatre, and the melodrama plays of the eighteenth century were tales of suffering, suspense, romance and evil deeds. Melodrama used music, special effects and dramatic scene changes, all aimed at thrilling and moving an audience.

The traditional melodramatic plot contained three elements:

◆ Provocation – the initial cause for setting the action in motion, very often the jealousy or greed of an evil character.

◆ Pangs – the suffering of the good and innocent characters in conflict with the evil characters.

◆ Penalty – the penalty is that suffered by the wicked character for his evil ways. He is usually caught in a last-minute reversal of fortune.

The characters

◆ Hero – handsome, strong, brave and honest

◆ Heroine – beautiful, courageous, innocent and vulnerable

◆ Villain – cunning, without morals, dishonest, cruel and evil

◆ Villain's accomplice – bumbling and stupid; the comic relief

◆ Faithful servant – comic relief and usually discovers evidence against the villain

◆ Maidservant – lively and flirty

Melodrama acting used strong facial expressions, large movements and well-projected voices. While this style is rarely used today, in the eighteenth and nineteenth century theatre, this style would be seen as a recognition of an actor's skill and success.

Melodramatic actors concentrated on showing emotions rather than feeling them.

It is interesting to note that some of the practitioners mentioned in Chapter 2 used the ideas of mask work and melodrama to create new styles of acting that we accept as the norm today.

Remember

The written examination is what gives you your grade for Knowledge and Understanding. Your teacher has already been continually assessing your Creating and Presenting grades. The three grades together give you your overall grade for Standard Grade Drama.

The Body of Knowledge

However, before we leave the topic of Knowledge and Understanding, and move on to look at the examination in more detail, there is an important thing to mention.

The Scottish Qualifications Authority (SQA) provides documents containing all of the course information that your teacher will need to fully prepare you for Standard Grade Drama. This is called the Body of Knowledge, and the exam markers also use it as a reference.

This document is available to look at on the internet but it is very long and was not written for students to use. The important points, which will help you achieve the best possible grade, have already been explained for you in this book. However, the Body of Knowledge does contain long lists of all of the key words used in the Standard Grade Drama course and it would be a very good idea for you to look at those carefully. The document can be found at:

http://www.sqa.org.uk

Select Drama from the list of National Qualification courses and then follow the link to Support Materials.

CHAPTER 6

The Written Examination

THE WRITTEN EXAMINATION

Introduction

You will sit two written exam papers. Every pupil in Scotland sits the General exam paper. You will probably also sit the Credit exam paper. The General is just there as a safety net in case you don't perform well on the day. The examiner will mark your Credit paper first. If you pass that, then the examiner won't even need to read your General paper.

The exam papers are made up of certain types of questions which come up year after year. In this part of the book you will learn about the most common and important types of question. You will have the chance to try some. All the questions are based on real Standard Grade exams.

Before we start looking at the question types, there are some important details to be aware of.

Key Points

◆ Each question usually contains a statement. Try to work out what the question is actually asking.

◆ Every question has a mark. The mark usually indicates how many pieces of information you should give.

◆ Sometimes the question will tell you what information to include. You must do this to get the most marks.

◆ The amount of space you are given to write your answer gives an indication of how much to write. If you run out of space you are probably giving lots of information you do not need to, unless your writing is really big. If you leave a lot of space then you have probably not answered enough, unless your writing is really small.

◆ Questions at the end of the paper tend to be worth more, so you may want to answer some of them first.

One good thing is that the first section of the exam paper is about work you have already done, so you can have all your answers prepared before the exam.

The best way to prepare for an exam is to practise answering old exam questions as much as possible. You should buy the published copies of previous exams if you want to do well. That way you are used to the style of the exam and there will be no surprises. The published exams have the answers at the back as well.

Format of the exam

The exam comes in two parts. Section A deals with your response to the stimulus that the SQA sent to your school a few months before the exam. Section B asks more general questions about the knowledge you have gained over the two years of your course, and gives you scenarios and situations to apply your understanding through planning on paper.

Section A

Your class should have been working on the stimulus for the past few months. A copy of the Stimulus paper will be provided with your exam paper.

Usually there are five pieces of stimulus. As previously stated, stimulus can be any of the following:

- A script
- A photograph
- A picture
- An object
- A piece of clothing
- A phrase
- A sound
- A piece of music
- A poem
- A topic

You should have taken one of these pieces of stimulus and developed it using your Creating and Presenting skills into a Performance.

You may have only performed to others in your class but you will have done enough to write about it. You may also only have been able to think about and plan theatre arts/production skills rather than apply them. That is acceptable for the exam.

In all your answers you should try to give reasons for your decisions.

Let's look at some typical questions.

1 **What ideas for your stimulus did you have?**   (3 marks)

2 **What ideas did you choose?**   (3 marks)

These two questions seem the same but they are not. The ideas you have might not be the ones you eventually went with. In your answers you should try to briefly state why you went with your final choices.

Hints and Tips

Do not just say that something is more interesting. Try to give a real reason such as that it allowed all the members of the group to perform; or it was an issue I thought was important; or we wanted to have a variety of characters.

Keep your answers short but clear.

3   What was the plot/scenario of your performance?   (5 marks)

Here you should state the beginning, middle and end of your play. You should try to mention the theme as well.

4   What was key scene in your play?   (5 marks)

Every play has something important happen in it that changes the plot or makes the audience think. Remember in Chapter 3, when we talked about narrative, there were five key elements:

◆   The Situation

◆   The Complication

◆   The Development

◆   The Climax

◆   The Resolution

Usually a key scene is either the Complication or the Climax.

Describe that event and then clearly explain why it is so important to the play. List the events leading up to it and the result that comes from it. If you can also tie it into the theme then that will also help.

5   Describe an important character in your performance.   (5 marks)

This question can vary slightly each time but it is roughly the same basic question. It can be about any of the following:

◆   An important character

◆   Your character

◆   A character the audience feels sympathy for

◆   A character the audience dislikes

◆   A major character

◆   A minor character

You need to describe the character as you have done in your character card. Try to then state why this character is important, sympathetic, major, etc., as appropriate.

6 **How was a character portrayed?** (5 marks)

Here you must list how you used your voice, body and gestures to act. It is very important that you state not only what you did but why you did this.

7 **How did you use theatre arts to improve your performance?** (10 marks)

This question can also be asked in a variety of ways. It might be a general question of how you would improve your performance, or it might ask you to use specific theatre arts.

Again, in response you should not only clearly state what you would do but why you would use these things. It is very important in this question to check how many marks are on offer as that will give you a clear idea of how many things to comment on.

8 **Describe your set or stage design/ground plan.** (5 marks)

There are important things you must include in any drawing design:

◆ It must be drawn as a 'birds-eye' view from above.

◆ You must draw the stage shape and the audience.

◆ You should try to label the stage type.

◆ You must clearly show the entrance and exits to the performance area.

◆ You must clearly show all set items, including flats, rostra and tabs.

◆ You should show the starting positions of the actors.

◆ You must include a key to symbols.

◆ You should try to label your ground plan to indicate what part of the performance it is showing.

◆ Your plan should be neat and tidy and easy to understand.

Now remember, not all these questions will be asked, and sometimes some of these questions may be in Section B.

Section B

The questions in Section B are harder to predict as this section tests your general experiences of Drama. However, as every student and class do slightly different things, the questions have to be open enough to give everyone a chance to answer.

Below is a sample of the kind of questions that might be asked.

Example

Give definitions of the following.

Corpsing:

Blocking:

Melodrama:

Theatre arts:

Mime:

Lighting grid:

The words will be taken from the Body of Knowledge published by the SQA, which was mentioned at the end of Chapter 5. The selection of words given here is only one possibility.

You will also be asked to write from your imagination and respond instantly to stimulus you have never seen before.

Example

Look at the following picture.

How would you perform this character?

You might be given a piece of script and asked how you might perform it.

Example

A: Did you get it?

B: No, C is bringing it.

A: They're late.

C: Sorry, my car needed petrol.

B: Is that it?

C: Yes, and you'll never believe what is in it!

A: I'll open it.

B: Wow!

A: What?

C: Told you.

Example continued ➤

Example continued

Continue the script. (5 marks)

Describe the relationships between the three characters. (3 marks)

Choose one character and describe how you would portray them on stage. (8 marks)

You might also be given a longer piece of writing.

Example

You are given a title 'The Environment'.

You have been asked to devise a performance with that title.

Describe in detail your performance ideas.

Include any or all of the following:

Plot/narrative

Characters

Themes

Performance styles/acting

Staging

Costumes

Lighting

Sound

Where possible try to list the reasons behind your group's choices. (15 marks)

In every one of these questions, you are being asked to put into practice all that you have been doing in Drama class and the skills you have applied for Creating and Presenting.

If you have applied the knowledge in the previous chapters then this should be no problem.

Remember

Keep your answers clear and specific. Make sure they answer the question.

The number of points you make should match the marks available.

Justify your answers where possible.

You will still meet questions that do not fit the areas covered here. There are simply too many ways a question can be phrased to cover them all. However, you should now have a good idea of what to expect.

You must try as many examples of past examinations that the SQA published each year. If you can not obtain these, your teacher should be able to give you copies.

You will no doubt also be working on past papers in class.

If you are really nice to your teacher, he/she might even mark some of the attempts that you have done outside class; your teacher may well be pleased that you are doing extra work on your own.

CHAPTER 7

Next Steps

NEXT STEPS

You should now know how to pass Standard Grade Drama.

So what next?

In school a Credit pass in Drama means you can move on to the next level of National Qualification. This is called Higher Drama.

It has four areas of study:

◆ Investigative Drama
◆ Study of a Text in its Theatrical Context
◆ Contemporary Scottish Theatre
◆ Acting

This can then lead you to study Advanced Higher Drama.

It has three areas of study:

◆ Devised Drama
◆ Twentieth-Century Theatre
◆ Drama: Special Study

You can also move on to study Drama at university or college.

Standard Grade Drama offers you skills that you can use to support other subjects.

In Drama a core skill is working with others, and this is a skill you will use in all aspects of life.

Drama helps develop your confidence and presentation skills.

Hopefully, and most importantly, Drama should show you how learning can still be fun.

Appendix

Key to Symbols in Stage Design

KEY TO SYMBOLS IN STAGE DESIGN

When designing a stage, it will be helpful to draw a ground plan showing where the exits, furniture etc. are located.

There are special symbols for several of the items you may need to include in your ground plan. These symbols should always be used in your sketches to mean exactly what they are called in the list below.

If you need to draw another item that is not in this list, you can invent your own symbol for it and add it to your own stage design key.

Flat

Door Flat

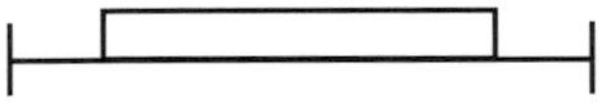

Window Flat

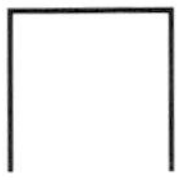

Chair

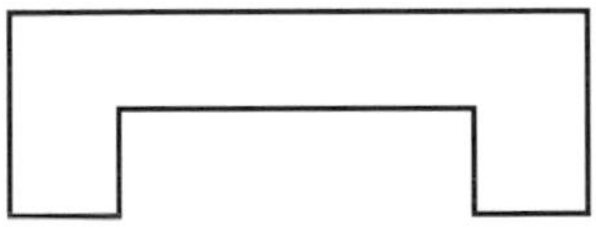

Sofa

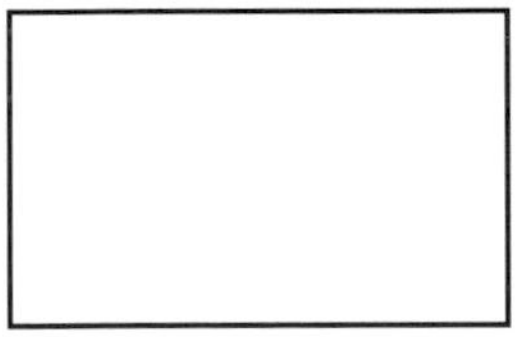

Table

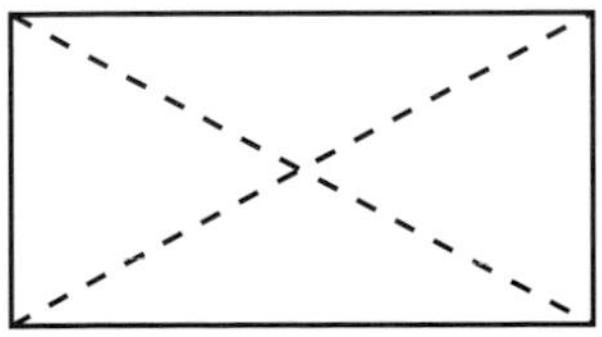

Rostrum

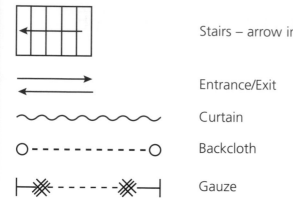

Stairs – arrow indicates up

Entrance/Exit

Curtain

Backcloth

Gauze